Introduction

What lies before you is all that I am - my thoughts, experiences and everything that I have felt during this strange period of my life that we call adolescence. I am young, 19 at the writing of this, thus wildly inexperienced in almost every aspect of life. Through the written word, though, and other forms of artistic expression, I feel grounded and confident in my abilities as a creator, though what I have yet to learn is both without an end and unknown to me. My love for writing dates back to my later years in Elementary School in which I would frequently write of worlds and places of magic populated by epic battles and such, which are common things to consume a twelve-year old's mind.

I read books of this genre for inspiration, such as Christopher Paolini's *Eragon* and T.A. Barron's *Merlin,* dreaming of one day writing an epic fantasy and becoming a world-renowned author. While this dream still holds strong in my mind, my preferred genre and current goals as a writer have shifted drastically, as my focus is centered now around poetry and works of literature with a more realistic storyline.

This shift into poetry began roughly two years ago, during my junior year of High School, and what truly peaked my interests, luring me further into this form of writing, was an author's ability to tell such a deeply rooted story, or express a complicated set of emotions, in so few words or with the use of carefully chosen descriptive words. Poets such as Longfellow, Thoreau, Emerson, and of course Shakespeare, have all inspired my writing and continue to feed my eternal hunger for new ways to express feelings and more effective ways to tell stories.

This collection includes different styles of both writing and poetry, but they share the common goal, though, of putting into word my thoughts. They are representations of my emotional mind, a place that is different for everyone, but one that universally experiences feelings in no particular order, the reason for my pieces being sorted in no defined sequence. In one moment, you may feel sadness, and the next moment may bring an overwhelming sense of joy that carries both your smile and energy. We all experience highs and lows, there is no denying that fact, but with age, through my own experience that is, comes an extended time in which those emotions remain with us, often going days feeling nothing but a void in the place where your heart should lie. And, when the things that we desire most are felt, the time in which they reside in us is almost cut short, and the cycle continues, endlessly repeating. This growth in both age and my emotions is both evil and good. An evil in that I have felt what it is to know nothing and be emotionally drained, but a blessing as well, for it has given me the opportunity to capture those emotions in their many layers and place them upon paper for the eyes of others to read.

Similar to other poetry collections, the entirety of this can be read in a single period of time, that is something that is completely out of my control. Perhaps these words will have but a minimal impact on your life, or maybe they will resonate deeply within you. All that I ask of you, the reader, is that you read with some intent. This does not mean for you to analyze each and every piece with a great depth, only that the words are taken in and allowed to sit within your mind for a moment. I wanted to ensure that these writings were the best forms of themselves, thus I revised and edited with the same care that I wrote them with, and I hope that these words, even if a single sentence, reaches some part of you.

The Slow Poison

I know of but a single remedy to rid me of what I feel inside
A cure for all sickness even
But I dare not find myself holding this vial
My hands cannot cradle anything of value,
Let alone something that will aid in my suffering
So I believe that my eyes have seen something
A moment in a life before this that doesn't allow me to possess this cure
A remedy for something only temporary in nature
But as is life, so what does it matter?
Take away what will heal, do not what I know will help, only to perish at a
moment untimely?
In time it will come, with a final setting of my sun
I simply do not have the luxury of feeling that release,
Not now that is
Not from the cause of mine own hands
My life is not my own
To hold and to cherish is not a responsibly of mine
Others make it somewhat valuable; they deem what is to become of me,
not I
It never could be
The remedy sits just out of reach
And I could cut my limbs, damage myself further to take hold of this elixir
But I will not, I cannot
For I am locked in a cage constructed by people my heart holds close
Because a life is not in possession of the one that lives with it
It lies in the arms of the watchers
How I wish to take it from them though
I feel what it burdens me with, do I not?
They know nothing of what a void does within a person
Dissolving slowly the meaning behind living
And the medicine meant to heal the wounds has lost effect
Or perhaps I have become immune to such fragile attempts

Maybe I'm to be forever trapped in this cage
And those closest to mine heart have given up
If this is what I will know for the rest of my days
This to be the truth the deceitful lips speak
Then so be it
I will wither away with time
This slow poison will do for now

The Wild Things

Protect the things that are wild
That which flows free and shines brightly, like a child
The chatter of white water in a rushing brook
The petals of flowers that the wind took
Movement in the hand of a painter
Songs of the voices born in a manger
For what is caged has lost its meaning
Locked and enclosed, what is no longer dreaming
So protect the things that are wild
And let them roam free, like a child

Of Dreams

Crawling upon the walls that build with slumber
are dreams of venturing to worlds unknown
Images that burn like embers
Clinging to us like a threaded needle, Sewn
into the fabric of youthful desires
But the cloak of time we wear to warm us in sleep,
Distinguishes the coals that once fueled our fires
And, it is known to all, age cares for dreams like a wolf counting sheep
But still we fall in slumber, and dream of places
that cherish the feelings our world retires
And we hope not to wake, to stay in stride with dreams' paces
But alas, the cloak of time puts out the soft embers of our fires

The Vacancy Of Gold

And I could paint one thousand skies
Fill them all with purple and pink as seen on the eve of nights
Gently lay myself down
And brush upon the canvas, white clouds
But not a single one
Would have a sun
For the light inside of mine own heart has gone cold
One thousand skies without their gold

Efflorescence

My eyes may dry and sorrow fade
She came with calm and timely care
The opening bud my heart conveyed
And thus, it blossomed there

Every Color but Bright

the pines roared in the night
a fire that burned every color but bright
no one could see the flames stained red
no one could feel the heat as it spread
but the fire was there
leaving most broken and scared
for the pines roared in the night
a fire that burned every color but bright
there were clouds filled by smoke, but there were no ashes
soon though, I found matches
someone had struck against a rough surface
leaving the rest in pulsing flames, a strong current
I followed the footsteps left in the ground
leading me away from all sound
trying to find who conjured the spark
that burned everything in the dark
the imprints were new and deep
and scattered about, like walking in sleep
but how could anyone be unconscious?
Breathing in this smoke so thick, it was toxic
from the pines roaring in the night
a fire that burned every color but bright
I then found an end
the footprints stopped at the forest bend
and I found you there
curled up, holding yourself in fear
I saw the box of matches
and next to it the pile of ashes
I walked closer to your figure
kissed your forehead and said in a whisper

"come with me, my love

smoke still falls from above"

your gaze turned up at me
the depths of your eyes as though a sea
and spoke in a soft voice
lungs filled by smoke, not by choice

"I set the pines aflame in the night
burning every color but bright
because I needed your saving
and you saw me before, but a wild thing not worth taking
so I set the world on fire
hoping the universe would take head of my prayer
to be protected by you
and loved, by you
every match
was struck upon memories of our past
when you and I once were
a love perfect in every way, but with a blur
I left the tracks for you to follow
hoping you wouldn't find me and think me hollow
so I waited here
facing these ashes was like looking in a mirror
because I burned everything for a chance to be safe with you
but I set flame to everything in your life too

I felt my eyes wet with emotion
at the thought of her burning in the open
waiting for me to save her
and revive all that we once were
I embraced her lips in mine
and felt movement at our fault line

"I loved you, from the day I saw your face

and upon leaving your grace
I never stopped feeling this way
but I felt I was lost for words to say
we were drifting apart
and I thought it best to be separate hearts
but hearts meant to be one
return always, to where they started from
I needed a light, something to act as my guide
but I was cast aside
and could think of nothing to do
to help you see my love anew
that's when I saw the pines, roaring in the night
burning every color but bright
I ran to them, to you
as I got closer, the flames they grew
my love, you did not burn my life
you returned to me my sight
allowed me to find you again
you who could leave my heart void of pain
I love you
And I still do"

I held her as she held me
our blur was now clear enough to see

we stayed underneath the smoke-stained stars
looking upon them as though they were ours
while the pines roared in the night
burning every color but bright
chaos surrounded us
but our hearts were in no rush
to leave this place
where we finally felt, safe

and there we were
together, while the world burned

Numb

     I cling to the small moments of happiness that enter my life, but alas that is all they are, only moments. They last no longer than a passing breeze dancing in the clothes of those it reaches or the fire upon dampened wood, for if they remained it would mean that I am happy, that I feel the warmth of its glow. I find that my own mind is neither content nor is it in a state of sorrow, I am more so not able to feel anything, as if my emotional bondage to life has been erased entirely. My decisions rest with nothing I feel has a great importance- doing things but without care of what I do them for. No single thing has a meaning that is of any significance to me, that is aside from sleep, the only part of life I somewhat look forward to. Being unconscious means you are unable to feel, like a glimpse of death but without the permanence of that voyage.

     I used to question frequently the meaning of all of this, on why we exist or what we exist for, but no more. My wonder has faded, as has much of what used to make me, me. I mean as much to the world as a single leaf that falls when autumn takes it from its barren branch; as much as a single rose in a field of equally fragrant flowers; an inkless pen in the possession of an artist. If my leaving were to take place, then it would matter not for life would go on, and I know this because I have felt what it is to be alive but with a lacking presence, I have seen that all I know does not stop simply because I cannot continue.

     I hold on to the singular moments of joy that enter my life as they come, dancing hand in hand with the wind as it passes or soaking in the droplets of gentle sunlight, tucking them away in envelopes for my drenched eyes to read later, for I fear that one may be my last.

A Dying Light

Let their thoughts be filled with agony
It would heal my mind from the splintered wood of this towering pine
And when the pain is cleansed and no longer a part of me
Return the cries, I will bury them and give them the last light of mine

Only Her

I have felt so much in so little time, devouring this lust and filling until I
can no longer hold it within my heart
But shallow am I to think of this as simply affection, for it builds
continuous and towers far above my weathered eyes
My neck cranes to see where she lies, but her figure is hidden amongst
moon and star
But I still believed that mine own heart could safeguard hers, but fools
only believe in ludicrous endeavors such as this
And I am that fool and every fool, venturing beyond every horizon to
reach her
But as sure as I am that the sun will rise and set again, I know that she is
too far to grasp, too fragile to protect with my callused and broken hands
Oh, but how beautiful she is, celestial does no justice to her allure
Bless what made her for they carved with close eye when she came to be
Her lines so delicate, and her brow never bending in anger nor frustration,
though sadness can be seen underneath, it had resided within her for a
time longer than should be in anyone
Still she is without flaw or fragmented beauty, even in anguish her eyes
shine like sapphires in burning light
Perhaps this is why her heart has ventured farther than my blistered feet
could carry me, as when in sadness, I never truly could protect nor aid her
from what she felt
When I attempted to feel as she did, approach and speak with kindness, I
saw only her and could gather no words to say, helplessly unable to offer
aid of any kind
I saw only the golden strands fall and silently rest in front of her eyes
Only the lips that parted gently at the crease, speaking words that her
graceful voice guided
Only her ocean irises that, when caught in their gaze, could turn a
hardened man into a wobbling wreck
And I felt all of this in so little time,

I have devoured my love for her and filled until I can no longer hold it within

Perhaps not being able to grasp her silk like skin is a virtue, in a cruel way, at least this is what I tell myself.

But as she lives and breathes in my presence, my need for air lessens, and I could perish at her will and never feel the slightest thing

She deserves far more than I could ever give, greater men are fit to bear her own heart,

For I was brought into this world only to witness such a jewel and feel its awesome power.

And I truly feel nothing else, nothing has meaning when my lips speak her name, or my eyes meet her own.

I just feel her.

Dark

The dark of my heart has been shown to no one
I would not burden them with such anguish, such sorrow
Without breaking though, I will die by the hands of no one
But I say once more, "I shall wait until tomorrow"

Darker

With my cracked palms pressed against my eyes
Chafing and damaging my sight
The ground beneath holds my cries
For my love of life no longer resides

Of Life

I once loved you
Although I have doubted
Time made it true
But I cannot hear how you once sounded

Field

in a field
that's where you found me
running
away from grey masses
for my storm was fast approaching

your arms opened
taking me in
and you held on to me

I hadn't been this
close
to someone for so long

my face buried in your shoulder
I cried
the same time the rain came
and you were there
holding me
alone in a field

I was no longer running

as time went on
this field became
our haven
we lay underneath
the afterglow of daylight
embracing the feeling
of just us

we talked about

all that we could
we laughed
when I needed it
and you kissed me
when we ran out of words
we stayed
there, in that field
I can still recall
for a moment too short

clear skies
soon had company
but they were so far off
I thought nothing of it

until the air became
tense
cold
dark

I ran
away from grey masses
my storm was moving
faster than before
and I reached for you
tried to grasp your hand
but you weren't
there

in a field
that's where you left me
running
away from my storm
and the rain came

but I had no one to
hold me

Blue Jay

Ever since I was old enough to remember anything, I had always felt trapped inside of my own body, never free to roam the world outside

I felt as though I was looking only down upon myself, floating just out of reach

This was comfortable for a time, for I was always there to watch myself, never going too far from my own beaten path

But time goes on and it changes that distance.
I live now on a perch above all things, far-removed from myself, and I hate all that I see.

I become saddened by what I am, every detail in every inch.

I'm there but not there, present and never conscious, and I know that this cannot continue, not for the rest of my life that is.

That's what I have to look forward to? The rest of my life?
If this is what it will be, then I want nothing of it- the distance from myself will only grow.

Grow until I am so far from where I was that I no longer am anything.

Take whatever I have left and bury it now, because although damaged, it's pure.

Whether I speak to a god, the universe or no one at all, take it now.

It's me in every way it can be and allowing the dirt to accompany what it is will give it peaceful rest. You mustn't touch nor move it.

For what I can recall, the purity that comes with happiness doesn't last for long, so I'd rather bury and protect it while it's still there. To take it with me would only let it die out, its fate to simply become another feeling.

I'm taking what remains, everything I hate, and will carry it over my shoulders with the anchor of despair chained to my legs, the song of the shackles to remind me of what I leave behind.

For the rest of my life I will take what I don't love, but at least as time goes on, I'll float further from myself, in time I will have to feel no more.

I look down upon myself, from this perch above all things, and watch as I bury all that makes me smile, screaming for it to stop.

I can't hear it.

I don't want to.

I carry the hate of myself with all else that brings me sorrow and anger, hoping that one day it won't mean what it does in this moment, that I can be the cure for this festering wound.

Time changes things- this is the only thing I know.

Whether I speak to a god, the universe or no one at all, take my mind and leave my body.

Bury whatever is left of me.

There isn't much, but it's pure. It's all that I have left.

Tsunami

It began with a peaceful current,
Your lips pressed against mine own,
A pulsating rhythm of breathing
In and out
In and out
But delicate.
The waves did not crash,
Rather gracefully fell upon the sand,
My hands caressed your warming body.
All at once the tide retreated silently
As our clothes fell to the floor,
Without a sound,
Two waves that were once headed for shore
Now crawling upon one another.
The current continued to draw back
Further and further
A rhythm once calm now growing,
Your breath on my skin,
Our moving with one another.
There was no storm
There was nothing but the ocean.
Nothing else in the world mattered,
Only you and I,
Alone in this moment.
A surge of movement could be felt under the surface
A depth no one could see,
That only we could reach,
Under tangled sheets and between our bodies
Nothing would reach us.
A current once growing was now powerful
Racing back and forth, a rising heat could be felt.
Oxygen was slipping through our hands

So our breathing became more intense,
In and out
In and out
We could see the peak of the wave
But it was in the distance,
Far from us.
The water rose,
And then it fell
Rising and falling, again and again.
The wave started to turn onto itself
Your back now pressed against the surface,
Our eyes were closed,
For we were going underwater.
The swell then collapsed forward
As my lips brushed against your neck
Then embracing yours.
The tide did not slow,
It moved rapidly, growing in force each moment
A pulsating rhythm passionately sustained between us both.
The surf rushed forward
And you held on to me as we came ashore.
The surge began to lessen slightly,
Slowly returning to a state of calm,
Small waves lightly touched the sand again
As I gently met my lips with yours.
For the ocean was undisturbed once more
It remained this way through the night,
As lunar rays lay upon the surface of the crest,
And you and I remained in sedation
Soon, you drifted off
And I followed,
Our bodies interlaced
As though we were afraid that the night would take from us the other
So we held

Between us this surge
Two currents that now could not survive apart

The Song of Us

With mine own shoulders and heart weighed down by this burden
A sadness without compare carries my words
I must allow myself to let wend of this love I know uncertain
And lay to rest our final verse

Tomorrow's End

I will hold thee in my arms
As though tomorrow is meant to burn
I will keep thine heart from harm
For our field smolders, and our flowers turn
Rain will fall, and with it the stars
The fabric of life may be torn
But I will hold thee and keep her body warm
For tomorrow is meant to burn
And yesterday is a place of no return

The Flood

My clouds were once sustained far above solid ground
Held up by serenity
By you
I was at the center of them all
Comfortably surrounded
By enormous arcs towering over my head
If the choice was mine, I would have remained
But I began to notice a change
The brushes of pink and red had faded
Overtaken by a grey hue
Flashes of light breached through my cocoon
A rippling roar followed each
The grey soon was stained with black
Both scattered about
It was then that I felt the first droplet of rain
I was still drifting, but held afloat with unease
I soon realized that I had been trapped
Within a storm
Completely surrounded by enormous bodies filled by dark emotion
I was no longer in the center, no longer in the eye
For then this place would be calm
The sky sparing only a drop or two
But I fearfully met downpour
It was deathly cold
The rain that bounded down like shards
The screams from the clouds deafened me
The flashes took from my sight
And the air thinned with each passing moment
I was fighting desperately to breath in her atmosphere
But any hope of salvation was far from reach
I was helpless
But in a moment, the clouds dissipated

Vanished completely
My body suspended by nothing for a moment
Before I was violently pulled down
And descended towards land
But as I fell
The wounds from the storm began to heal
The sound of the wind rushing passed soothed my ears
And the air that flowed in quenched my lungs
Although I healed, my falling did not slow
The ground became painfully clear
And I had no arms to fall into
Thoughts of an end occupied my head
For I could not stop myself
What could I do?

You once held me afloat
Kept me safe above all things
And I was surrounded by your grace, an eternity all too short
For time became less of a friend to us
You poured yourself onto me
And I could only fill
And I did this without release
Immersed in water and surviving only just
You angered when I would not listen
Became frustrated by my lacking response
But my ears were deafened, and my lunges flooded
You thought that I had lost sight of us, of you
But my sight had been taken from me, I was blinded
The empty hole inside of me filled without end
The echo of my voice lost in the rushing water that poured in
And you left

For a time, my mind was clear
Staying afloat in the shallows with ease

I came to know serenity once again
What I once felt with you
And the scars from my wounds began to heal
But I soon realized that I only needed time to breath
That I never wanted you gone
Foreign was the land I bounded towards
I had forgotten what it was to live without you
But what could I do?
You left when I convinced you that I didn't care enough
But truly, I could feel nothing within myself
I have never loved anyone as I did you
And without you here
I have no one to fall into
No arms to lessen the impact
Nobody's eyes will open to my descent

The ground was closing in
It looked, different
It had been so long
For the clouds you painted had always been above it
A place where I once knew serenity
And you were what held me up

With All My Heart

With the eyes of mine set upon yours
My lips part to make my passion heard
The words I speak could mean no more
Although they have been deferred
With all my heart, I say to thee
I love you, and I have felt no other
My hope in hand to make you see
With all my heart I will love no other

Frigid Air

There is a frigid air that follows the night when it comes
A fragrance of moonlight and skies filled by stars
Flickering orbs resting gently above reflective clouds
Planets that shine just the same

Craving attention.
Meteors are seen ripping through empty yet filled space
A shower as we call it
And we find beauty in this

These things that remain suspended in dark matter
So far from us all
We call beautiful what is unknown to our touch
But what lies underneath is our hatred for it

The unknown things that we can't
Hold or feel
This is our glacial air
That follows the setting sun

The night is brimming with scenes of allure
A blanket of moonlight to cover the earth
Constellations imprinted on the black canvas
Jupiter and Saturn fluttering far from us

We wear broken lenses to see this beauty
But the scene quickly disappears
Like a setting sun
Like the night sky fading into day

This hate crowds our empty yet filled minds
And all that we can think of,

All we may hope to feel
Is our frigid air

Thread

I once believed that everything was good, that what I saw and felt could never lack a sense of joy, that all was left unstained by the deep hues of hate. But as I've gotten older- *no I'll rephrase that, for it sounds as though I blame maturity for this-* as I've become more conscious in this world- *yes, that sounds better-* all that I've known has slowly lost what I once believed it had. The goodness in things has soured in my head. Nothing ignites the fires of my imagination anymore, not like when I wasn't as aware of purpose, before I had been shown what the world drew depicting good and evil, and maybe it's my own fault for letting it slip through my hands. *Couldn't I put this on others though? Blame the world for taking away this joy I once knew? It wouldn't be fair, I know that, but it would give me some relief from the load I carry upon my shoulders, because as of late the weight grows upon every exhale of mine.*

Each day I tread a little further into fear, dreading the thought of living yet another day, always yearning for my eyes to close so I no longer have to be conscious, to live in my dreams and experience life like how it was meant to be felt- *not free of problems, of course, more so with little worry.* I look at myself in my ever-shattering mirror and watch as my smile becomes weaker, harder to hold up for others. That smile is for those in my life, so they don't have to worry about keeping me afloat, though the surface is one that I know less each moment. I try to make others laugh, make light heart of a moment when I can, simply because I never want another to think something is wrong, have to deal with my own mind and what it feels. There is enough wrong in this world, and I would rather not add to that towering mound.

My closeness to very few is comforting- *one person that is* -but is also worrisome for me. The closer someone gets, the more I may show and the more they will see, a picture I would rather not paint in front of anyone but my own gaze. Someone, though, opened my eyes to a new world- *the world that I dream of, if you will-* and I in those moments with them completely forgot anything was wrong or could ever be, my paint strokes flowing freely, without fear to guide them- *I believe it to be anger as well, but anger comes from fear thus the seed in which all others root.* They gave me something for my mind to focus on, introduced me to things other than worry, a pattern of notes that I hadn't heard before. Their existence made mine a little easier to bear, for my smile had never been so weightless, my laugh never so present, and this was felt only with them- *for a time I truly thought I had been dreaming.* I became afraid, though, when they got closer, enough to see more of me, to feel the paint rather than watch from afar. I took myself away from them, distancing myself in any way that I could- *I stayed a little quieter some days and blamed it on a lack of energy or said that other things occupied my mind and were distracting me* -all because I didn't want to become so close that my heart latched onto theirs, believing it needed another's life for survival. I couldn't let something break inside of me and release onto them, for we were now close enough to damage. It wouldn't be fair to them or I, as they would have to choose whether to help or cast me aside, and I would have to live and die with that decision.

 Why would I take that piece of my mind and lay it to rest on them when I could simply add it to what I carry? There is enough wrong in this world, and I would rather not add to it. And I would have broken by now if the weight was too much to hold up, so what is one more thought of pain going to do?

 People always ask how I am, the most common, common courtesy question we know- *to start what I call "surface tension conversation"* -and always I say what they want to hear, give the same mindless answer that we all have tucked away- *"I'm fine" or "Oh, you know, the usual", whatever that means* -for I don't want anyone to deal with what I feel, no one should have to. But today, my smile was weaker than it had ever been, and I tried to make it better, attempting to raise it with the much-used thread and needle, but I didn't feel anything. I tried to make myself believe that everything around me was good, that nothing could ever be wrong. And, as I do to those I meet, I lied to myself once again.

To a place

I can take you with me if you'd like,
we won't stay for a time longer than we are meant to,
for I don't want to hold you back from the rest of your life.
But I could take you with me, to a place with mountains and the tallest
trees,
and a lake.
Each day, we would feel the wind brush upon our skin,
wade in calm, lapping water warmed by the waking of day and let the
current hold our bodies.
In the dark of night, we would lay in open fields,
watching as the sky becomes the resting place of stars and planets,
bodies that lie out of reach but shine no less brightly.
We could be free and in love,
away from everything and everyone.
It would be only you and I.
So I could take you with me if you'd like, to a place for only our eyes to
see, only ours to feel,
a place with mountains and the tallest trees,
and a lake.

Heal

Rest without disturbance, mine own love, and awaken tomorrow
For the night is frigid, and it is long
Peradventure the hours shall carry away thy sorrow
And the nightingale heals thy wrongs

All Within a Night

Yesterday I could feel you, but today there is nothing. You allowed that love to fall through your fingers and seep into the cracks of the floor we balanced upon.

The flower that latched its roots into the soil upon our meeting is now bending at the stem, letting go of the petals that make it so. If the ones who gave it life become distant, you and I both water and light, it can live no longer than a moment's passing. And I, I cannot give what is left of me in nourishment, for it would surely drown.

The final leaf was carried away by a gentle wind in the night, the same moment I felt my love for you vanish completely, and the rising sun dried what remained of it. Our flower died, and with it the memory of us, all within a night's passing, and today I feel nothing.

Smoke

Smoke invaded my lungs
It crowded every space where oxygen once resided
And I was surrounded by flames licking my skin
Imprinting themselves where they saw fit
I could not move
My hands were chained to my feet
Completely helpless in a house, burning to the ground
The crackling of wood echoed in my ears
And I could see the smoke rise
For I was watching from the outside
As I was burning
I stood away from that house, watching myself smolder alongside fragile wood
My mind was horrified the longer it remained in sight
My ears assaulted by my own screams
But I could do nothing
For I set aflame the house I built
Smoke filled my lungs as it burned down around me
And I stood outside, watching myself burn

What the Darkness Taught

Sometimes when I'm alone
I feel an overburdening sense of sorrow
And it is not something I can rid myself of with a forced smile
Or a thought of happiness
It stays for a time longer than I would like
But sometimes it's not so bad
Occasionally I want to drift along this river Anguish
It is not that I wish to be saddened
More so because happiness and whatever lies in between
Isn't appealing
It can become hard
And this is when I think of not being here
This is not to say I'm suicidal
Only that sometimes, it's incredibly dark
And when the light is that low
You begin to wonder if it ever was a part of you
You think that maybe you weren't here at all, not really
I don't want to leave them though, the dark places I go to
I'm frightened of turning back
For when I leave, I know that I'll return
In time
The process will repeat, turn on itself once more
And I will be immersed in these thoughts again
I'm okay with that though
And that confused me once
Because I was afraid of the dark
But it held no fear for me
And when I came to know that,
When I came to understand that it meant no harm
I wasn't afraid
It helped me understand that
Not seeing anything is clearer than the life I'm living now

So maybe it's a good thing
Being without a light for a time
It only confused me because I was never shown this place
No one ever tells us of it
Teaches us that this darkness is real
Because most believe that when sadness is felt
When a blank stare is all that we have to spare
We want the beating of our hearts to cease
But in truth, I just need a place to go that isn't here
To do what the dark taught me
And not see for a while
So I turn out the light
Or it fades on its own
And there's nothing again
But sometimes my dark is too dark

Balance

All that is good must come to an end
And that which ends must be good
The rushing water at a river's bend
The hummingbird that hummed all that it could

I cannot say when time takes this final breath
Only that all good things must come to an end
The forest roots must dry after its final sun has set
And so will it too, upon the time of men

For all that has been, and all that is good,
The rain as it brings a thunderous cloud
And all that is understood,
Everything must make its final bound

Salt

My feet have stood upon burning sand, scorched by the midday sun, but no pain was felt through my fragile skin. The wet breeze cast from afar, beyond a horizon that I have not seen, healed whatever was torn and broken within mine own heart, dried the sorrow that crawled from mine eyes. The waves play a game with those who stand ashore, running to and fro weathered feet, toes sinking further below tiny rocks, as though playing along. This playful nature revives the life that I once knew long before this moment, filled with joy and smiling faces, for this is why I stand upon the sand.

As it runs back and forth like children in an open field, it is also strong-willed and full of a might unmatched, perhaps why we find ourselves gazing upon it for hours and never feel fatigue in our stare, for it is ever changing. We cannot hope to understand it- it's movement and pulsing rhythms- and this is both its allure and what instills fear in our minds. The beauty in what we don't understand and a subsequent fear that comes with these obscure things.

Although we do not truly know the nature of the sea, it knows of us, our thoughts, wonders and angst are not hidden from the shallows. This is why I, and many, may stand upon blistering sand and feel nothing but a sense of wonder, as the ocean reveals none of its secrets. Each time I return to the shore, more of its beauty is sewn into my heart with a delicate needle, a process that will take a lifetime. Never will we truly understand what the ocean means to do or see its many depths and learn the waves we will not. It will continue to sew its fabric upon each return, and only when my end is reached will the piece be finished. Only when death is where I drift will I see the depths of the sea.

Beauty

What is beautiful is not ageless
What is beautiful is not tameless

The flowers are not free from damage
The vines do not climb unmanaged

Love is not without changing
Love is not without hating

That in which beauty lies
That, which is beautiful, dies

Youth

"You'll never be this young again". A phrase that I have heard many times, and one that both frustrates me and animates dull thoughts within my mind. The nature of its annoyance comes from the generation of people that experienced youth in a time long before those of us today, for they are who spoil the meaning behind all that it is and means. It's not that I lack an understanding for finding a worthwhile endeavor to pursue, for being able to support yourself independently is a vital aspect of this society, and one that mustn't be overlooked. What angers the mind of mine, one that age has barely embraced, is the idea that regret is all that will fill my dreams in a later time, that I will find myself longing to be young again, to feel youth's kiss upon my lips as I lay with lost time. But as I ponder on this, there is no way to feel that sense of freedom while young without having some form of regret upon the coming of old age, so what is there to do? Is being young defined as choosing the turmoil we will experience in a later time? Many tell us to not worry about what the future holds, but how can we not? It worries me, someone who has known life only briefly, that I will be regretful of this precious time, one that I was able to fully take hold of, but I find myself caught between living freely now or locking my wishes away and releasing them later.

I have taken away the sense of accomplishment I once felt at a much lesser maturity, upon finishing a work of art or even writing, although they fill me with joy, they do not immediately progress me in any way towards living in a state of stability. This is as much my fault as society's strange view on what real work is defined as, what is worthy of doing in the eyes of the masses. This process of falling into a state of anxious thoughts drains me, everyday filled with worry of what my future is meant to be, if what I am choosing to do with this time is right. The pedestal I have placed my hopes of living freely in youth has been demolished by my constant anguish and worry over what my future self will think of my actions, what I didn't do or could have done. I have no grasp on what youth truly means, or if it means anything at all only that it belongs to me. What am I to do with it then?

Unnoticed

I frequently wish that I had been born without anyone knowing of my existence, almost born into a dream, venturing through life on the shoulders of freedom. I could do what I wished with no one to tell me otherwise, no one to criticize my actions, for they would not know of me. I would like, though, to still be noticed by the things of nature, for they fascinate me, they excite my mind. The trees, clouds and animals I would desperately wish to still feel and see, and for them to notice me. I have been told, taught even, that the leaves on a tree or the blades of grass, each with their own shape and color, are simply there and nothing more, that they exist but offer nothing further than a lifeless presence. When I raised the question, "But what if they feel?", I was ignored and looked over, like the leaves on a tree or a blade of grass. The scented pines, the cool rushing river- nothing in nature turns their heads upon my existence. Rather, when my throat is dry and my tongue is cracking, distant waters roar to assure my senses that they lie not far from my own. And when the sun becomes painfully overbearing, heavy upon my shoulders, and my skin begins to welcome a new pigment, the leaves of an oak rustle in a gentle wind to let my burning skin know shade is not far off. Never do they refuse to offer help, after all we have done to them, not for them, and never do they ask for anything in return, only wish me safe passage through this life.

If I had lived in this world unnoticed by man, each morning, as sunlight shot through closed curtains and found rest upon my drowsy eyes, I would listen and know that the birds sing for my own ears, as I exist only to them and they to me. Of course this is untrue, for they know all men, but I wish it were only I that they saw, because as the world moves forward the birds still sing gently, but are unable to breach the ears of busy people, all but mine. I have noticed this, though, that they sing without hope of praise or recognition. Perhaps they have become used to the silence that follows, the same silence I have known all too well, the reason as to why I can hear them so. I often wonder if they wish to leave this world, as I do, if this lack of appreciation takes somewhat of a toll on their spirit, longing for praise in another place. For even when snow falls and their voices can be heard no more, man seems to notice not. But as we remain in the cold air of winter, the complaints of the chill falling just as heavily as the snow, the birds seek warmer weather so they may return to us and awaken the buds of spring.

We call ugly the barren trees of winter, the yellow of the dormant grass and the sharp wind that blows, but we judge too quickly and fail to appreciate the life hidden in plain sight. The seeds of fallen trees and lilacs that have reached their end lay underneath the soil, kept alive and well by the fallen treasures of Autumn and Winter, and upon the soft heat brought by Spring, the melted frozen droplets seep into the soil, and it awakens once again. All that went away returns; the rushing water in a babbling brook, the blades of grass upon rolling hills, the leaves that rustle in a gentle breeze, the bees that hum and buzz, the flowers that bloom with a warming sun, and the songs of birds when morning light creeps above low lying clouds. All of nature returns and displays its charm without praise from us, without hope that we will acknowledge all its beautiful things unveiled, for it knows better than to rely on the word of man.

I often wish that I had been brought into this world without anyone knowing of my existence, except for the things of nature. I would gaze upon its pallet with delicate care, dance joyfully along with its songs, and praise each second of its existence, and it would do the same of me. Of course, this will never come to pass, but at least I have learned this: Foolish are those who rely on the word of man in this life, and more foolish are those who seek their praise.

Air

you tell me
to breathe
to take in
what is my
air
but my lungs
remain empty
my heart beats
without it
so I'm just
there, floating
surviving without air
you tell me
to breathe
but it does nothing
if you're not here

Summer Love

I pray that on Autumn's day
I do not stray far from your gaze
For fallen leaves do not bring
The same melody that Summer sings

On a Ledge

I'll hold on with this loose grip of mine to what is left for me to take hold of, but oh, how I have wanted to let go. Every fiber within me, every voice inside screams notes of profound dissonance, but they cannot resolve themselves in a way that makes sense, as though they know I'm not supposed to do this but cannot find a reason strong enough to convince me otherwise. My body dangles from this ledge, the tips of my aching fingers and my fear of being this far above ground being the only things prolonging this fall, but I could do without this fear, do without my conscious telling me what I should and shouldn't do. It often feels as though another person, my mind and I two separate beings trying to control one heap of skin and bone. They argue constantly, mislead each other with words, breaking down further and further a trust built over time, and the older I've gotten, the more they feast on their own lies:

"You're fine", one will say, "You're not hurt, I see no wounds, so why do your eyes fill with sorrow? You shouldn't feel like this, not if there is nothing to feel, it isn't right. It isn't fair of you."

Then, with some usual hesitation, the other attempts to rebuttal, "But, I suppose he could talk to someone, no? Is he not right to do so? He once felt something just as any other, so why can he not?", the other will turn his head away in disgust as though forcing himself not to listen. Again though, the one that questions speaks, "I have seen him happy, and it is something of great beauty, and I have watched tears fall from his eyes just the same. But now, it is as though he feels nothing, but everyth-"

"Enough", the other interjects with a rising anger, "Of course he feels, would he wear this face of sadness if he were empty? He doesn't need anything from you let alone help from another. He's been given his share of chances, someone else deserves it now."

"But-", the questioning one stops himself, unsure of his words and fearful of what the other will think, "Couldn't he-", and again he stops. After some thought and a dread filled stare from the opposer, he walks off and leaves the other alone, in control. Soon after though, he too leaves the dimly lit room, a place filled with nothing but towering walls and empty space, the echoing footsteps of their leaving bounces from wall to wall for a time too long.

Those two exist within the confines of my mind, and they argue and control, exchanging roles constantly but never long enough for me to become familiar with one of them. One forces me to look down at the safety net which is the solid ground, and it turns my stomach to look at the sight of such an end. The other, the one that questions, tells me to look up with hope, but the uncertainty in their voice makes me only look upon what I have left to climb, the extent in which I must travel to save what is left within me.

There is a third voice, the one who looks and cannot decide, who sees a desire in both letting go and holding on. This is the one that lives and breathes through my lungs, moves with my limbs, he who goes between knowing stability and being cruelly unable to hold his own balance. Although he lives in me and I in him, I drift towards all of them at different times, for I am each of them and none, taking sides with whichever entity I feel can control the moment. They all talk at each other, not with, until one's voice is too overpowering for the others to take, often becoming painfully loud and venturing into the hours that belong to sleep.

This time, though, they shout and scream, but there is no resolve. No voice is louder than the other, and the one that can't decide is fighting both the pull of gravity and the rigid ledge my fingers take hold of. I must remain here until they tire themselves, the ones that violently yell, talk at each other and never listen. What other choice do I have? I've been holding on for far longer than I had intended, listening to them argue with such rage, and I am unsure of what will come next, if I should let go to silence them or reach for safety. I don't know what will hurt more.

I'll remain here on this ledge, alone but in painful company, until some unsettling agreement is conquered. It's not so bad, you become used to being this alone, on these broken ledges, when it's the only place you have left to be.

The House That Life Built

I drank a poison
From a vial that held within
Waters that death ruled
But I returned, only to tread in life

I placed a gun against my head
Loaded within its chamber
A power to destroy the mask of life
But I came back cloaked in death

I placed a rope around by neck
Tying a knot that wrapped around
The tree that life swings from
But I returned, only to be a puppet of death

Each time I disrupted the balance
Leaned more towards life or death
One fulfilled the other
And I always came back, maintaining the balance

Upon each return, I was someone else
Not happier, nor anymore distraught
I wasn't in control, no more than before
But I kept returning

I ran from the house that life built
Returning only to be welcomed by death
I was born from death
Only to die in life

And each time,
I came back

The Thief

I have never truly lived in this world
My body lies in another place, curled

Awaiting my heart's return
But that land will never again be heard

I died some time ago
In a field of flowers kissed by gold

There, I drank freely the air
And let the days pass with little care

I strolled through meadows that shined
Reflecting the light of a sun divine

But one day, I came upon a rose
Its petals were draped in red velvet clothes

My eyes were strangers to this color
And without hesitation or a thought filled mutter

I clasped in my hand around the stem
And tore it from the ground it peacefully lay in

This was when life deserted me
Like a man of work giving their final heave

Holding in my hands the heart I had stolen
From my field of gold, I thought it would not end

My body still lies among the gentle spoken larks
While my mind lingers in this eternal dark

For I died some time ago
In a place kissed by the sweet lips of gold

I took what was not mine
And gave nothing of myself in return for this find

That place is now without a heart
The thorns of the rose left on me its mark

The punishment I must wear
For choosing to act without care

Who I Have Loved

Who I have loved is someone of false existence, they have never known life, not really. I came to know and understand this upon my descent into the heart of another, or that which I believed it to be, but as time in this world moved forward, I realized that it wasn't theirs. I was aware that I hadn't been made to live in their heart, never were we meant to care for each other in this way, as much as I desperately wished it so. Confusion took hold of my life for some time, not knowing why I felt this way for someone so different than I, our lives as though a nightingale to the mourning dove, both sharing this life but with different flight and song. Although her face acted as the hawser that pulled my ship through this barren sea, I understood that what I had felt wasn't for another, rather I had been in love with the concept of loving, holding deep affection in my heart for what planted that feeling, not who. I still think of her when affairs of my heart are known, for it was she that I saw when I first came to this foreign place, when I first felt true love. Others have worn this mask of what I believe love to be, being almost real at times but quickly returning to my mind as a memory I have not yet known. The one I knew first comes frequently to try it on, the mask, though always it cracks or shatters upon the fragments of my heart, for I know that she could never be. Still I try.

I believe that one day this idea of love I have constructed will take a tangible form, though when or who this will be is unknown to me, as it is to whom this feeling will rest in. Time has ventured further into the light we cannot see, and I look upon both love and loving as two separate beings, both having a need for my arms to connect them, to create a bridge for them to once again embrace each other. Without care for myself though, that bridge will never be, love and loving can never know of each other if I do not heal myself. I will not know the care of a stranger if I know nothing of my own heart.

I can remain in this place though, at least for a moment longer, content in the knowledge that who I care for has never existed, being no more real than the love I show for myself. I may continue to live this way, to be only a small piece of this world as though a nightingale that sings from dusk until the gentle light of dawn, holding in my heart a deep affection for this concept of loving and being loved, an idea I do not yet understand thus one that I cannot care for. As I drift along this barren sea, she still pulls me forward, the one I knew when I first came to this place. And although I do not know what love truly is, where it lies or what form it takes, I know what it feels like. It felt like her.

A Final Thought

Hope is what fear let slip away
And fear is what hope could not save